Contents

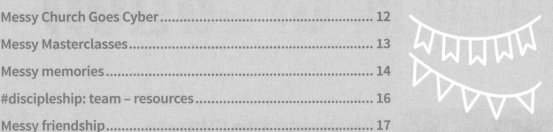

Session material

What do the different parts of the session mean?

Messy health check: As part of your team planning, share thoughts and feedback about your Messy Church and congregation.

Messy team theme: With your team, choose one or two key messages to focus on.

How does this session help people grow in Christ? Is everything theme-connected and helping all ages to be more like Jesus?

Mealtime card: Reflective questions to consider during mealtime conversations.

Take-home idea: Continue family activity/exploration between sessions.

Question to start and end the session: Use on social media/posters/flyers too.

Social action: Link the theme with additional activities, charities and events or explore international issues.

Go to **messychurch.org.uk/getmessysep21** to download all templates at A4 size, including a session planning sheet.

If you are using these sessions for a Messy Church at home, look out for this symbol! These are activities that can easily be adapted to the home.

In our next issue

Caring for creation

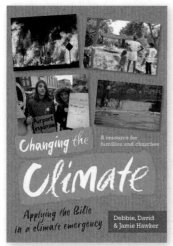

ISBN 978 1 80039 022 5, £9.99

Changing the Climate

From Debbie, David and Jamie Hawker, a family taking action for climate justice, this workbook shows links between the Bible and environmentalism and how we can all play our part in climate action. It's great for engaging families with the Bible and motivating them to take action.

A Christian Guide to Environmental Issues

Environmentalists Martin and Margot Hodson explore eight environmental issues, including climate change, food and population, and share why and how Christian faith and concern for the environment should go together.

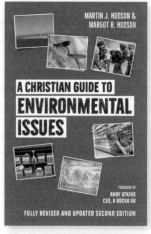

ISBN 978 1 80039 005 8, £9.99

ISBN 978 1 80039 068 3, £8.99

Green Reflections

In this beautifully illustrated gift book, Martin and Margot Hodson bring together scientific and theological wisdom to share biblical reflections on the environment and how we should look after the world we inhabit.

Order at **brfonline.org.uk**

Lucy Moore writes...
The present of the present

I've been pondering on making the most of the here and now, of the present of the present. It's been miserable being in such a long pandemic situation – and for many people it's been more tragic than merely miserable. It's been a privilege to help assemble the stories of the beautiful Messy Church leaders who have moved on to their seats at the great, Messy table waiting for them just out of our sight (page 14). They are deeply missed, but we rejoice in the gift of their presence in our network and the privilege of sharing our time on this planet with them.

It has been tough, very tough, and we're not out of the woods yet. But here we are, at the turn of the seasons, placed here and now for the here and now in a here and now that is unique. No time has been quite like this. And God has chosen YOU to be the people to deal wisely with this opportunity! The verse echoing round BRF over the past year has been: 'And who knows but that you have come to your royal position for such a time as this?' (Esther 4:14, NIV). There is no getting away from the fact that, in God's eyes, YOU are as good as it gets for the here and now. YOU are like Esther – vulnerable, perhaps; feeling inadequate, perhaps; pant-wettingly scared, perhaps – but nonetheless the right person in the right place at the right time for whatever God wants to do next.

> **You are the right person in the right place at the right time for whatever God wants to do next.**

It's a moment of transition. A watershed. A short season when the choices we make right now in September, October, November and December 2021 will shape the next season of kingdom-growing in the countries we live in. We've had an unprecedented chance to let go of the unhelpful aspects of the past and we've been given space to consider what we really want for the future. Will that be backward-looking? A nostalgia for everything to be as it was? Or an excitement about the present and future, now that space has been cleared for change to happen? Will we dive straight back into the old ways?

Or will we demand of our church councils that we *don't* unthinkingly restart everything that was there before? What could we leave buried in lockdown in order to invest more in what will liberate more people into the freedom of a life with Jesus? (If you don't, who will?)

One of the uncomfortable challenges that's been whispered around Messy Church for years, and which has been reiterated in the *Voyage of Discovery* report about deepening discipleship in Messy Churches, is the challenge *to let go of something* in order to have more time and energy to invest in your Messy Church, so that people have even more opportunity to become lifelong followers of Jesus. Once we restart all the old and beloved groups, habits and practices in our inherited churches, our time will fill up quickly, unless we deliberately claim the time for what we really long to do and be (or should that be for what God really longs for us to do and be?). At the very least, it's a chance to talk as a team about what your Messy Church is actually for and to shape your ministry from now on around those aims. If we can't do it here and now, we're never going to do it: this is a once-in-a-lifetime opportunity.

So my challenge to you and to myself is to take some time in the next few weeks to continue your conversation with God, or to start one, asking the Holy Spirit to shine a light on anything you need to lay down and to warm your heart around what you need to take up for the sake of Jesus and of those who don't yet know him. It sounds weird to say it in the context of this magazine, but if that means laying down Messy Church, that's what you should do. If it's laying down something else equally loved, have the courage to do that – for such a time as this.

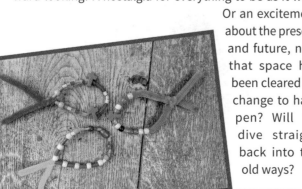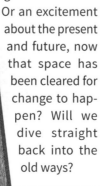

United States

Creativity in the USA

Johannah Myers

In the US, Messy Church is creatively adapting to the pandemic challenges and finding great gifts in new ways of working together. Local Messy Churches continue to find new ways to gather together. Messy Church at Community UMC in Huntington Beach, California, has led the way in online Messy Churches – even figuring out how to share a meal together while they meet virtually. Families can sign up ahead of time and have pizza delivered to their door just in time for Messy Church! Other Messy Church communities have created fabulous Messy Adventures for families or family pods to enjoy together outdoors. More about those Messy Adventures can be found on Messy Church USA's website at **messychurchusa.org**.

As an organisation, Messy Church USA continues to grow. Like the UK, we've recently moved from having Regional Coordinators to growing a team of Messy Ambassadors, people who are passionate about Messy Church and sharing our Messy story. With our Ambassadors and our Board, we've created five new teams to address the growing needs of Messy Church USA as we seek to equip Messy Churches in the US to start, sustain and connect.

Denmark

Messy Church in Denmark

Karen Markussen

2020 was the most silent year when it came to Messy Church in Denmark. Most communities have been totally closed, and contacts and meetings with families have not been able to take place.

But in Vigerslev Church they endured the challenges by sending Messy Church online once a month. They made short videos with greetings, activities, songs and a celebration. There has been great feedback from the participants and for them it was joyful to have something going on, while so much was still closed. Many of the participants contributed to different elements throughout the meetings. They look forward to being able to meet physically again. It is incredible how God uses different people and their abilities and resources to keep this initiative going.

Australia and New Zealand

Celebrate and rejoice!
Messy Church in Queensland, Australia

Dianne Natt

After eight months of only being able to connect with our families online, Messy Church at Bayside Uniting Church in Brisbane, Queensland, was able to come together again in person at the end of November 2020 for an Advent picnic. The families brought their own picnic dinner and picnic rugs, and we enjoyed carols, craft and games under the trees on a warm summer evening. Special woolly visitors to our picnic were lambs, Starlight and Blu, carefully watched over by our shepherd, Revd Craig.

It was with much excitement that we were again able to reconnect with our Messy Church families for our Australia Day social evening at the end of January. There was much fun with obstacle races, thong throwing, wet sponge challenges, craft, family charades and, best of all, a fabulous BBQ dinner.

Covid regulations were closely adhered to at both events with regulated sign-in, hand sanitising and social distancing where possible. God has blessed our Messy Church with wonderful families, a committed team and a safe environment in which to meet. We are so very grateful.

Refresh the Mess – Australia and New Zealand conference

Melissa Neumann

On Saturday 21 February 2021 we held our second national Messy Church conference – except we held it online across six time zones! Tech was hosted from Western Australia. Speakers were from South Australia, Queensland, Victoria and the UK. Conference artwork was provided from New Zealand. Over 120 participants came from all around Australia and New Zealand, and two from the UK!

We lamented the past year, shared stories of new opportunities, celebrated God continuing to be at work through Messy ministries and were resourced through workshops on being intentional about discipleship processes and re-engaging with volunteers and families. Lucy Moore closed our conference with the encouragement to consider how the five values of Messy Church shape our Messy Churches and the challenge to give God control and move with God's Spirit, like a surfer riding a wave, to experience the fullness of God's grace moving through Messy Church communities.

The feedback so far is that people are 'pumped' for a new year of ministry!

Latest research on Messy Church and discipleship
Six discipleship approaches in one research project

Claire Dalpra

In the recent research on Messy Church, entitled *A Voyage of Discovery: Deepening discipleship in Messy Churches and beyond*, findings are six-in-one. Or one-in-six. Six discipleship approaches piloted in one research project and one report presenting insights from all six. Funded by the Church of England, 24 Messy Churches tried out these approaches with Messy Church leaders as the local experts, supported by BRF and Church Army's Research Unit.

One. If there was one headline I would draw out across the entire research, it would be the priority of making time for team reflection. Ask one another, 'Where do you see God at work?' We aren't practised enough at asking this question, but sticking with it takes teams beyond whether there were enough sausages to what matters for deeper discipleship.

Six. What insights from the six approaches? For **Faith conversations**, while tempting to try in your existing gathering, it proved a richer experience working with a smaller group at a separate time. For **Social Action**, don't underestimate the value of memory-making as families work together to help others. For **Messy Extra**, the importance of leaving space to see where God takes informal conversations with families. For **Maturing Teams**, how swiftly the dynamic changed for the better when teams began regularly reflecting more deeply together. For **Peer Mentoring**, the power of God at work in one person's life to impact a group. For **Young Leaders**, the upside-down, humble way adults need to be open to learn from teenagers just as much as teenagers learn from adults.

How can I tempt you to delve into more of the insights we uncovered? Like a sort of bingo challenge, look out for *glitter*, *Marmite* and that well-known board game *Mouse Trap* in our findings report. But on a more serious note, prayerfully read through the voyage of discovery these amazing leaders have been on – the highs and the lows – and reflect together which of these six might be a right direction for you.

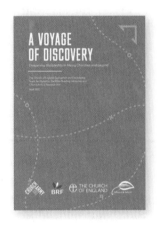

messychurch.org.uk/
deepening-discipleship

Messy Church Goes Wild!

Lucy Moore

We've been increasingly interested in the way Messy Churches can help people grow closer to Jesus through the natural world in all its many forms. Lockdowns meant that we could be church outside more easily than inside, so many Messy Churches reimagined their presence as outdoor garden-, graveyard- or street-based events.

We've always been aware of how important the natural world is to children's spirituality, how important the care of the planet is to younger generations in particular and how much we can all learn of the creator through the created world. But there's also been a growth of understanding about the concept of 'wilding' or 'rewilding' in the church more widely – giving the Holy Spirit more space to act and being less controlling or more open to being surprised by what happens when we are wholehearted about putting things into God's hands.

So over the next couple of years we're making space in Messy Church to encourage a sense of 'wildness'! It's about opening up possibilities, firing the imagination, providing helpful resources if and when they're needed and sharing the failure and success stories compassionately. It could simply involve more encouragement to use sustainable materials in your Messy Church. It will be about sharing stories of how to meet outdoors and about the reimagination of our five values with particular reference to the world outside church walls – places, people, plants, animals, landscapes. It will also – we hope – involve the total being greater than the sum of the parts. In other words: we'll be doing things together that wouldn't be possible if we were on our own. Exciting times!

Messy young leaders

Dylan Heydon-Matterface (aged 16)

The last year has undoubtedly been difficult for everyone, myself included. After the UK prime minister's announcement of lockdown in March 2020, my peers and I initially felt ecstatic to have the chance to potentially miss weeks of schooling with few ramifications. As everyone tried to get on top of how to teach and study online, I stayed positive, looking forward to the fact that 'everything would be back to normal by Christmas'.

I'll admit, right from the start, I had my doubts about whether this really was such a good thing, but I remained hopeful and kept looking forward.

As days turned into weeks, and weeks turned into months, things definitely started to go downwards. It became increasingly obvious that the time missed from school would, in fact, impact on our futures, and a growing sense of unease emerged in us all. Our teachers started piling on the work more and more, and I became fed up with having to spend increasingly long hours at my desk, with a fog of uncertainty blotting out the final goal of exams.

It got hard at times, especially having to worry about whether or not our GCSEs would actually go ahead. The significance of the schools' closure was becoming incredibly evident. The monotony really brought me down: wake up, get ready, spend most of the day in front of the computer, eat dinner, then back to sleep.

As we slowly started to trickle back into classrooms in September, things were finally starting to look up, at least for the time being. The daily routine that had become rooted deep within me finally changed somewhat, but it was still very regular and uninspiring, as so many pursuits remained unavailable.

So when the opportunity arose to get involved in the Messy Church young leaders group, I jumped at the chance to add something interesting to my weekly schedule. More than anything, it was an excuse to exercise my creativity, which had been dormant over the preceding months. It brought a breath of fresh air into my otherwise stale mornings.

Dedicating a short amount of time in the month to dream up interesting crafts and activities was decidedly

> I jumped at the chance to add something interesting to my weekly schedule

rewarding. Thought-provoking discussions encouraged me to think of new ways that I could rejuvenate my own life: each session left me motivated to not only put my creativity into action but also generally feel better about myself and to be more positive to those around me. The effort required to prepare all the necessary paraphernalia beforehand was more than justified by seeing people genuinely enjoying the activities we had organised. It was very fulfilling.

Our Christmas session was especially memorable. I created a festive greetings card during the session, which I gave to my parents afterwards. It seems mundane, but in 2020 even the smallest things could cheer me up and give me the encouragement I needed to keep my head up, to keep looking towards the eventual end of the worrying and concern.

Above all, opportunities to express myself and carve my own path are what I've missed the most over the past twelve months, as the tedium of online academia eroded my enthusiasm. I'm massively grateful to my fellow Messy Church young leaders for the inspiration and motivation I needed in these trying times, and I look forward to many more successful online sessions.

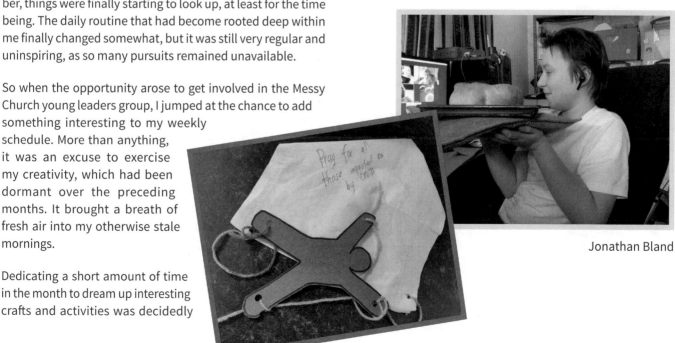

Jonathan Bland

Meet the support teams

Our new support teams are working really well! Meet some individual team members and find out what they do and how they can help you.

Pool of Wisdom team

Hi, I am **Charis Lambert**, one of the leaders of the new **blue team** – also known as the Pool of Wisdom. We are here to use our experience of Messy Church to plan, organise and deliver events and activities to support the Messy Church network. Each blue team member has many years of Messy experience in many different places and varied contexts, so together we have a wealth of ideas and innovations! We love to hear new ideas and help others to begin new Messy things too.

Our first main focus was the Messtival in May 2021. The morning was for all leaders and teams, with training, seminars, workshops and discussions. In the afternoon we hosted the Great Big Messy Church, providing the activities and the online celebration.

If you have any ideas about ways that we can support you in planning Messy events on a large scale, do get in touch. We can share our experience of Messy Meet-Ups, Messy Camps, Messy Cathedrals and indoor and outdoor events. If we can't help, we will know someone who can!

Alongsiders team

Hi, I'm **Mel Cleveland** and I'm part of the **purple team** – the Alongsiders. We are here to encourage and enable you wonderful Messy leaders. I know from experience that running a Messy Church is both a joy and really hard work – sometimes it feels like you have to keep all the plates spinning. Phew!

At times, it's good to step outside the stressful situation and talk it through with someone else. Some things come more naturally to us than to others. When I get too busy, I'm hopeless at delegating, thinking it's easier to do it all myself – big mistake, and not good for the rest of the team, who would probably love to help! But now that I know I do this (thanks to talking this through with someone), I can do something about it.

The purple team members have all received training in how to help you when you come up against a knotty problem or want to do things differently. So why not sit down with or Zoom someone from the purple team and get a fresh perspective? We don't have the answers, but we could be part of enabling you to find the right answer for your particular situation.

Trainers team

I'm **Dawn Savidge**. The **red team** (no, we don't all wear red) – the Trainers – are all passionate about Messy Church and about providing you with excellent training. The season of lockdown gave us all a chance to re-evaluate what we do and it was with that in mind that we wrote a series of Messy Masterclasses. These training sessions give an opportunity to reflect on where we were pre-Covid and mid-Covid and where we can strengthen, reshape and relaunch post-Covid – whether that is more intentionally including discipleship, reshaping to meet the current needs of our families or including young leadership roles into the heart of our team.

I have loved the sense of community in running the Reimagining Masterclass. When you get a bunch of Messy Church teams in one room, the ideas and conversations just flow. You can feel the atmosphere lifting and people being inspired to try new things or move in a new direction. So far, we have run both the Reimagining and Discipleship Masterclasses; we also have a Masterclass on how to start a Messy Church. My prayer for you is that you continue to press in to God's vision for your community, even when you can't quite see the road ahead.

Messy Church International Conference
20–22 May 2022
Key international leaders, 23–24 May 2022

Making a difference!

It's going to be a particularly exciting International Conference next year after the many months of missing out on human contact. We're so looking forward to meeting new friends from around the world and catching up with old ones. Yes, there will be a packed programme to equip and inspire us all to do our Messy Churches even better, with the Messy Church values making it a welcoming, creative, Christ-centred time, bursting with fun for all ages.

We're very excited that our main speaker will be the amazing Paula Gooder. Paula is a speaker and writer on the Bible, particularly the New Testament, and is currently Chancellor of St Paul's Cathedral in London. She'll bring a lifetime of study and expertise to our main sessions. So there will be plenty to exercise our brains and stretch our thinking.

But there will also be plenty of space to hang out with people and just 'be'. The international planning group is keen for us to make space for refreshment within the programme, whether that's giving permission to go and sleep off your jetlag or staying and having a long coffee-time chat in the lounge without fear of missing out on something vital. You'll be so welcome, whether you are new to Messy Church or have been part of the network for years.

Who is the conference for? Anyone interested in Messy Church from any country, who's old enough to help on a team. (Depending on individuals, around age 8 upwards – all under-18s need to be accompanied by an adult.)

What can you expect? You can expect the conference to make a difference to you, as you catch a vision of where God is leading you. You can expect it to make a difference to your Messy Church, as you return to it brimming with confidence and new ideas. And you can expect it to make a difference to other delegates from other countries, as they learn from you in return.

Book your place at **messychurch.org.uk/MCIC22**.

Snapshots from Messy Church International Conference 2019

Now available:
Messy Discipleship

An in-depth exploration of how Messy Church is addressing the discipleship question

£8.99
from **brfonline.org.uk**

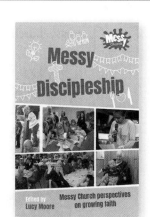

Now available:
Messy Vintage

52 sessions to share Christ-centred fun and fellowship with the older generation

£8.99
from **brfonline.org.uk**

Messy Church Goes Cyber

Vickie Heydon-Matterface, Derbyshire, UK

Over the last 18 months, many of us have been trying out new ways of being and doing Messy Church. Some of us have continued with a physical model of interaction, with Messy bags or drive-thru sessions. Some have even moved online temporarily, with a view to going back to the 'in-building' sessions as soon as possible, which mirrors the general pattern of church congregations all over the UK.

Unfortunately, some Messy Church groups have had to close for a variety of reasons, and there are numerous families who have simply 'lost' their Messy Church. These are the families who might choose to continue, or start, their Messy journey with **Messy Church Goes Cyber**: their local church right there with them in their homes and on their devices. For some families, 'in-building' church is not always an option due to a vast range of additional and complex needs.

The difference with **Messy Church Goes Cyber** is that this group won't be going back to the 'in-building' model. It is a new digital church plant existing entirely online. Monthly Messy Church sessions will happen via Zoom or Facebook Live, including all the usual features: intergenerational crafts, activities and celebration, encouraging interaction, fun, learning and storytelling. Videos will be published on our YouTube channel, so that a mixture of social media platforms can be used to maximise the interaction and learning opportunities.

It's helpful to think of public platforms like Instagram, Twitter and Facebook as a church noticeboard, where events and news can be publicised and basic information for families shared, such as how to access 'the church'. The real sacred space is contained within a Facebook group, which is private and served by a stewardship team of volunteers, just like more traditional church. These stewards help to keep the environment safe and welcoming, as well as facilitating discussions and conversations just like the discipling team leaders within regular Messy Church groups.

Alongside the monthly Messy sessions, families will be encouraged to journey together and grow in their Christian faith. Material such as Alpha, Messy Basics and Holy Habits can be accessed via learning blocks, so that families can work at their own pace and progress together. Discussion together and relationship-building is important and encouraged, along with opportunities to engage with local mission projects and eventually take on stewardship roles within this church and go on to mentor newer families.

How can you get involved?

- Do you know a family for whom this model of church would be beneficial? Refer them via email (they need to consent) and they will be contacted by one of the team and signposted to the Facebook group.

- Would you like to help write, record or plan interactive sessions to further explore different media platforms, such as an idea you tried that worked really well on Zoom?

- Follow us on social media and help to spread the word.

- Pray for the team and for the right families to find us.

 facebook.com/MessyChurchGoesCyber

 @MessyChurchGoesCyber

 @MCGoesCyber

 Messy Church Goes Cyber

 messychurchcyber@gmail.com

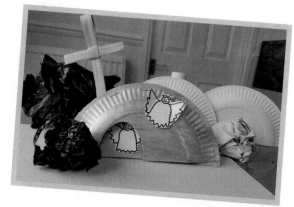

Messy Masterclasses

We're so glad to have been able to offer a rolling programme of online training on Zoom throughout 2021. The feedback from this training has expressed how much we all appreciate just being able to encounter others with similar concerns, even on a screen. We're particularly grateful to the Trainers team for their willingness to offer their time and experience to others in the network. It's been exciting to see online training happening in other countries as well – if only there was time to drop in on them all!

At the start of the year in the UK we focused on three topics: 'Reimagining your Messy Church' (by far the most popular, unsurprisingly), 'Discipleship in Messy Church' and 'Starting your Messy Church'. As the landscape changes, we look forward to expanding the range of themes in response to changing needs, so please keep letting us know what subjects you would appreciate Masterclasses in, so that we can shape what we offer to be as useful as possible. We have some great ideas already including 'Thoughts for the future', 'How to reengage with families when we can meet again safely in person', 'How to re-energise and build the Messy Church team within the church'.

Messy Meet-Ups online have also been a more informal way for Messy leaders to keep in touch. Do join in any time. The details for Meet-ups and Masterclasses can be found at messychurch.org.uk/upcoming-events. Thanks to all who have combined bookings with donations: your gifts make a big difference!

Almost everyone who responded with feedback appreciated the sessions. Here are some comments:

- 'Sharing of research and chance to reflect on specific situations.'

- 'The stimulus and challenge to think again and learn from others within well-structured, varied presentation from [the leaders], the opportunity to hear what other Messy Church groups have been doing in lockdown – and the openness with which all these ideas were presented so that I could think through what would suit our Messy Church at this time. Lovely to see so many people – lockdown can be lonely!'

- 'Very grateful for the thoughtful preparation and all the contributions from leaders and participants. This second lockdown period is harder than the first and apathy is lurking around the corner! It was so good to be jolted out of that and have thoughts and ideas sparking again. Well done the Messy Church team and BRF!'

- 'I came away from the session with joy in my heart and wanting to know more. Thank you.'

And my favourite piece of advice from a delegate (I wonder if our colleagues in other countries encounter the same thing): 'When sending complete strangers into breakout rooms, it's helpful to ask one person, maybe with a name that begins nearest the start of the alphabet or something equally easy to see, to lead off, otherwise people sit and look at each other in silence for a bit, all being very British and not wanting to push themselves forward, and so wasting valuable discussion time!'

Messy Memories

The last year has been hard and, for some, full of grief. Here we honour and celebrate those we have lost.

Parishioners and our Messy Church team were shocked and saddened when **Denise Vince** passed away on 2 December 2020. She was part of the core group that started Messy Church at St Matthew's, Hastings, New Zealand. Denise continued faithfully and enthusiastically to help plan and run sessions. We remembered her at a special time during our December 2020 session, giving thanks to God for Denise, whose deep faith underpinned everything she was and did. Looking around that day, we could see and feel Denise's influence and practical input everywhere. Here were her cushions, table coverings, the beautiful toys in our preschool corner, craft materials, posters and nativity costumes for the play. There will always be so many reminders of her enthusiasm for Messy Church, her love of the children, her imaginative teaching skills and her love and outspokenness for our Lord. Rest in peace, Denise, and rise in glory.

Revd Jane Holmes was deeply committed to her faith and the people of her parishes – those with faith, those with different faiths and those with no faith. She was happiest with children and loved baptisms, school and family services and particularly Messy Church. She revelled in the singing and the dancing, enjoyed the crafts and believed that eating together was a particularly lovely way to share, both food and faith. And the children loved her; school visits were accompanied by squeals of welcome – for a friend and a guide. Sadly Jane died in early 2021 after a long time of illness. We all miss her for she touched so many souls living here, way beyond and outside the walls of the church.

Jim was much loved by everyone, and with his friendly nature he quickly got to know people, not afraid to ask after people's faith and well-being. He enjoyed being the outside welcomer for families, always with a cheery greeting. He liked to help using his practical skills, encouraging us to have a go.

Jeanne joined the Messy Church team in our first year, and was a tremendous asset, giving encouragement, welcome advice and ideas. Even when ill she was determined to be at Messy Church, serving our breakfasts, helping at craft tables and joining in with our celebration time. One mum told me how Jeanne was always ready to listen and this has been true for many of us, as she asked about family members including pets, difficulties and happy times.

I'd like to pay tribute to a wonderful, servant-hearted, much-loved team member, **Jo Tyler**, who died suddenly of a cardiac arrest in hospital while being treated for Covid-19 in November, aged 59. Jo had served as our 'techy' man since we started Messy Church in 2014 and as such was a pivotal member of the team. Jo's life had been transformed by the power of God's love many years ago and he was always happy to tell others of God's power to keep and protect him throughout his life. Jo was committed, kind and reliable, going above and beyond to serve the team well. When we are able to meet in person, we will certainly miss Jo's input tremendously, but he will always be remembered with love and affection.

Linda Colson helped out regularly at Messy Church in Hornchurch over many years. The welcome and craft teams benefited from her wealth of knowledge, experience and patience gained as a primary school teacher and special educational needs coordinator. Retirement provided her with time to share these valuable skills and her faith with all ages at Messy. After moving to be closer to their family in 2018, Linda and her husband Ron became involved with church life in their new parish and continued to support our Messy Church with valuable prayer. In March 2020, God called Linda home. We were blessed to have known such a kind, friendly, prayerful lady whose beautiful smile and thoughtful words of advice and support are missed by all who knew and loved her.

Jenny Clarke was one of our core team right from the beginning when we started Messy Church in Hornchurch, ten years ago. Being a retired deputy head teacher and having 36 years' experience of Scout leading, she was the ideal person to lead the welcome team and interact with all ages. Her organisational skills were second to none. With her deep faith, wide base of friends and experience in pastoral care, she was able to talk to anyone, enlist new helpers and offer the right words of comfort and advice at times of need. In 2019, Jenny's health declined and she was no longer able to attend our sessions. She continued to enjoy being kept up to date about what was happening at Messy Church. Jenny died in May 2020 and is missed by her many friends and our Messy Church family. We thank God for her life and friendship.

Michael Wenborn was an avid volunteer, so when his fiancé invited him to come and help set out chairs for a Messy Church session, he came willingly. From then on, he always had a job of his own! Due to his speedy organisation of all that is required for 80+ people to sit down for a two-course meal, he was known as 'King of the trays' within the catering team! Michael is possibly our only team member to have spent time enthusiastically volunteering on so many different teams over the years: setting-up, catering, welcome and security, craft/activities, as well as the annual Messy Outdoors and the light party team. It was a privilege to celebrate his wedding to Kathy at a Messy Church meeting in 2018. Sadly, we lost such a hard-working member of our team in January 2021. Michael's cheerful willingness and happy smile will be greatly missed by all the team and families.

When we started Messy Church in a Prison, a handful of Messy leaders came forward, including **Gill Betts**. It was clear to the group that she would be the best person for the job and we voted her in! She loved the idea, but was worried that she wouldn't be able to do it, especially as she was also undertaking training for licensed lay ministry (LLM). I assured her that she would, and that we would be supporting her. Over the next few months as we met with the prison teams and had 1-2-1s together, it was clear that this ministry was a real calling for Gill, one which she could never have anticipated, but which God had revealed in his good time. It was an absolute joy to see this realisation dawn slowly on her as our Messy Church @HMPRochester opened. As Gill became more and more involved in other aspects of the prison's life and work, she recognised that prison ministry was her calling, which culminated in her LLM being licensed to this prison ministry and working with the prison chaplain. It was a blessing for me to play my part in her journey. Gill loved this Messy work, and was a blessing to others there. She is greatly missed.

#discipleship: team

Extreme... Crafts

Barry Brand

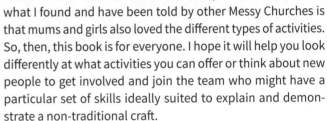

What a crazy time we've been living through. I'm writing this in February 2021, waiting for the next government briefing on the latest rules we need to follow, ever hopeful that schools will be open soon and we can meet up with friends and family. And of course, we hope we can run our Messy Church in the church building with all our Messy families. We've moved to doing Messy Church online and we gave out 'Messy Church in a Pizza Box' during Covid, but I, like all of you, am really missing that face-to-face contact, the noise, the chaos, the spillages, the homemade cakes.

I started to write 'Extreme Crafts 2' towards the end of 2019, before any of us had heard the word 'coronavirus'. I carried on writing at the start of 2020 and then the world changed, including, for many, meeting in churches. Creating a book designed to be used by groups meeting at church when most of us weren't allowed to was a strange thing to do. I guess it reminded me of the fact that the church is the people and not the building. I've added 30 crafts to the existing 50 from the first edition of the book and I think you're going to enjoy them. There's a nice mix of easy activities to do together and more tricky crafts, which can all be done at home or shown on an online Messy Church if we're still locked down. The crafts continue to be categorised like the last book as 'Arty', 'Big', 'Construction', 'Science' and 'Edible'. Each craft gives you a mess, danger and difficulty rating to prepare you for what's ahead as well as some helpful themes and things to talk about if you need them.

The first edition started out as an idea to try to get more lads and dads along to Messy Church – moving away from cutting-and-sticking crafts and instead going a little 'out there' – and this next edition continues that theme. However, what I found and have been told by other Messy Churches is that mums and girls also loved the different types of activities. So, then, this book is for everyone. I hope it will help you look differently at what activities you can offer or think about new people to get involved and join the team who might have a particular set of skills ideally suited to explain and demonstrate a non-traditional craft.

The main thing is to have fun. For a lot of people over the last year-plus, fun has been a little lacking. I hope this book will inspire you or reignite that fire to share the good news. Maybe you're still doing your Messy Church online, maybe you had to stop altogether due to circumstances or maybe you've been able to start up again in your church. Wherever you're at, be kind to yourself. It's been really tough for all of us, and it's easy to be hard on ourselves and think we should have done more or done things differently. We're not and never will be perfect. We'll always be a bit messy, and that's okay.

God bless,
Barry

The new edition of *Extreme Crafts for Messy Churches* is available on **brfonline.org.uk** for £9.99.

We wish you a Messy Christmas!

Find **Advent** and **Christmas** resources for your **Messy Church** at **brfonline.org.uk/messychristmas**.

ISBN 978 0 85746 091 2, £6.99

ISBN 978 0 85746 521 4, £2.50

ISBN 978 1 80039 018 8, £4.99

Messy friendship

Judith Moore,
BRF fundraising development officer

I read somewhere that once you've been friends with someone for seven years then you are friends for life; even if you fall out of touch, that friendship still remains. With Messy Church turning seventeen, we are sure there are many lifelong friends across the world and we hope for many more to come.

Friendships are very important to me, and the Bible also speaks about the incredible value of friendship. This is often overlooked, as the stories of family relationships in the Bible often grab the attention. But the Bible also has many examples of rich and powerful friendships. Take this passage from Acts (which is explored in the November session from p. 28):

> All the widows stood round [Peter], crying and showing him the robes and other clothing that [Tabitha] had made while she was still with them.
> Acts 9:39 (NIV)

Who were these women? They might have been women who had assisted Tabitha in her good works, but they could also be women she had helped – women with extreme grief at her loss as well as a clear desire for Peter to understand what an amazing woman Tabitha was. I would suggest that at least some of them would have called themselves her friend.

When Tabitha is raised from the dead, Peter makes a point of calling for the widows 'especially'. He wants them to know their friend is alive.

There are stories of friendship like this throughout the Bible, and the book of Acts is a testament to the value and power of friendship. Throughout the stories, we see person after person opening their homes to the disciples, allowing them to make their journeys spreading God's word.

In September 2020 we set up **Friends of Messy Church** as a way for people to give regularly to our ministry.

If you are already a friend of Messy Church, we want to take this opportunity to say thank you. Your donations not only help to fund our ministry but help us to plan ahead. If Peter were here, we'd be pulling out all the amazing things we have been able to do because of your help to show him: 'Here's this project; here is all this amazing training; look, here's this resource – this one is especially good!' Whether it has been seven years, seven months or even seven days, we are so pleased to call you friends. Your generosity allows us to continue our journey of helping people of all ages to hear the good news.

If you'd like to become a **Friend of Messy Church** by giving from £2 a month, you can do so by visiting brf.org.uk/friends.

Friends of BRF

Registered with
FUNDRAISING REGULATOR

> **We would love to hear from you...** even if you just get in touch to say hi! You can contact the Fundraising team via **giving@brf.org.uk** or on 01235 462305.

Session material: September 2021

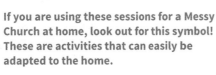

Go to messychurch.org.uk/getmessysep21 to download all templates at A4 size, including a session planning sheet.

If you are using these sessions for a Messy Church at home, look out for this symbol! These are activities that can easily be adapted to the home.

Bible story

Mark 10:46–52 (CEB)

Jesus and his followers came into Jericho. As Jesus was leaving Jericho, together with his disciples and a sizable crowd, a blind beggar named Bartimaeus, Timaeus' son, was sitting beside the road. When he heard that Jesus of Nazareth was there, he began to shout, 'Jesus, Son of David, show me mercy!' Many scolded him, telling him to be quiet, but he shouted even louder, 'Son of David, show me mercy!'

Jesus stopped and said, 'Call him forward.'

They called the blind man, 'Be encouraged! Get up! He's calling you.'

Throwing his coat to the side, he jumped up and came to Jesus.

Jesus asked him, 'What do you want me to do for you?'

The blind man said, 'Teacher, I want to see.'

Jesus said, 'Go, your faith has healed you.' At once he was able to see, and he began to follow Jesus on the way.

Pointers

The story of Bartimaeus on the surface appears to be a story of physical blindness and healing, but a deeper look reveals it to be a story of persistence, compassion for those on the fringes and new beginnings.

- Bartimaeus is an alternative disciple. He teaches the twelve disciples about faith.

- Bartimaeus was persistent. He asked more than once for what he wanted and what he needed. He was not deterred by the people shushing him. He was not afraid to seek something he needed.

- This is an example of Jesus having compassion and mercy for those who are considered 'less than'. He treated Bartimaeus, whom other people despised, with respect.

- Jesus teaches us to see the world with new eyes – to see and feel the world differently.

#discipleship: team

Messy health check

If nobody in your Messy Church seems to be desperate to get closer to Jesus, could you pray for some 'shouting'?

Messy team theme

- What amazing thing has happened when you have had faith in God?

- Have you ever been afraid to seek something you needed?

- Have you had encounters on your spiritual journey that have helped you see or feel differently about something?

How does this session help people grow in Christ?

In life we often beg and plead – having doubts that God will hear us or respond to our needs. All God asks of us is to trust. When we have faith in God, as Bartimaeus did, we are made whole. This session provides an opportunity to explore a fresh start, seeing the world anew, when we truly trust God.

#discipleship: families

Mealtime card

- Who are the people that teach you about faith?

- How do we help or hinder people from moving towards Christ?

- What does it mean to see something with new eyes?

Take-home idea

Who are the people in your community who are shushed? Say a prayer for them and end it with, 'Lord, in your mercy, hear my prayer.'

Question to start and end the session

So… what do you want Jesus to do for you?

#discipleship: extra

Collect used eyeglasses and send them to the nearest Lions Eyeglass Recycling Center.

Social action

Find a local organisation that advocates for those moving from homelessness to being placed in a home and give a 'shout out' on social media to bring awareness to their cause.

Trusting is believing by Leyla Wagner and Marty Drake

Activities

1. Obstacle course

You will need: anything that would make a good obstacle (hula hoops, caution cones, chairs, etc.); blindfolds

Place obstacle items in any order to create a path for people to walk through. Work with a partner. One person will be blindfolded and the other person will guide them through the obstacle. Once through, the partners can switch roles.

Talk about how hard it is to get around obstacles in life if you can't see. Bartimaeus had to have help getting to Jesus. He trusted that Jesus was God's Son and would help him. God is always with us and we can trust God to help us, too.

2. What do you see?

You will need: printed pictures of animals with different-shaped eyes; a picture of the night sky; a picture of the day sky

Set the night and day pictures on the table. Look at the animal's eyes. Place the pictures of the animals that you think are awake during the day on the day picture and the animals you think are awake in the night on the night picture.

Talk about how the shape of animals' eyes help them to see differently. Big and round eyes help animals to see in the dark. Almond-shaped eyes help animals to see all around them. Look at the shape of your eyes. What can they tell you?

3. Keep shouting!

You will need: coloured paper; pencils; a plate or other circular item for tracing; scissors; felt-tip pens or crayons; stickers; masking tape

Trace the circle on to the paper. Decorate it with felt-tip pens, crayons, stickers, etc. Cut out the circle. Roll the paper into a cone and secure with a couple pieces of tape. These can be used as megaphones in the celebration time.

Talk about how, when Jesus was leaving the town of Jericho, Bartimaeus began to shout to Jesus. Bartimaeus was overlooked by those in his town and had to be persistent to be noticed. Who is overlooked in your community and has to shout loudly so they can be seen and heard?

4. Snack challenge

You will need: round or square crackers; cheese slices cut into quarters; sliced cucumbers; hummus; blindfolds; plates; knives

Construct a snack sandwich while blindfolded to raise awareness and build empathy for those who are without vision.

Talk about how every day we complete tasks without even thinking about it. Bartimaeus relied on help from others to get to Jesus. Do you think Bartimaeus could have easily made a snack? Jesus showed Bartimaeus compassion and respect. How can we help those who are unable to see? How can they help us?

5. Hidden surprise

You will need: two to four printed pictures of optical illusions found on the internet (use Google or Pinterest)

Lay the pictures on a table for participants to look at and discover the hidden picture.

Talk about how something unexpected happened in today's story – Jesus heard and responded to a request from someone everyone else ignored! Are there people in your community who might be overlooked or told to be quiet? God wants us to see in new ways – to look beyond a first glance and to see and treat all people as God would.

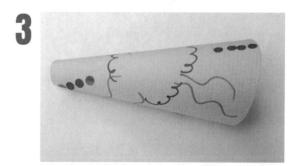

3

4

Session material: September 2021

6. Grab bag

You will need: blindfolds; a cloth bag filled with items, e.g. pinecone, fruit, toy cars, pasta, stones

While wearing a blindfold, one person takes an object out of the bag and uses their other senses to guess what it is. Let the person take off their blindfold and see if their guess is correct.

Talk about how people without vision rely on their other senses to help them. How do you think Bartimaeus felt about getting a fresh start – seeing things in a new and different way as he followed Jesus?

7. Reaching out

You will need: large poster paper; markers

Write at the top of the poster, 'What do you want me to do for you?' Trace your hand and write or draw a picture in it asking Jesus for what you need help with.

Talk about how Bartimaeus' trust gave him the courage to ask for help, and his faith healed him. Is it easy or hard to ask for help? Sometimes it can be hard, but God wants us to ask.

8. Persistence pays off

You will need: masking tape; straws; pom-poms

Place the masking tape in straight, curved and zig-zag lines, either on the floor or on a table. Give each person a straw and a pom-pom. Place your pom-pom on top of the tape. Blow it from the start of the tape to the end of the tape without blowing it off the tape.

Talk about how Bartimaeus was surrounded by people 'shushing' him, but he continued to call out for Jesus. God wants us to be persistent in our praying and seeking. What makes it hard to be persistent? What keeps us from asking for what we need?

9. Reading by touch

You will need: self-adhesive jewel stickers; Braille alphabet chart; Braille template (download online); paper; pens

Write words from the story, such as 'mercy', 'faith' and 'trust', on a paper. Using the Braille template, choose one of the words to recreate in Braille, placing the jewel stickers in the appropriate places. Run your fingers over the jewels to read the word.

Talk about how Bartimaeus asked Jesus for mercy. Mercy is compassion and kindness. Jesus showed Bartimaeus compassion by healing him. We may not be able to heal others like Jesus did, but we can show mercy to others. How can we show compassion and kindness to others?

8
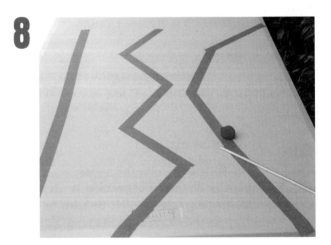

6

7

9

Trusting is believing by Leyla Wagner and Marty Drake

10. Bartimaeus in a bag

You will need: two lolly sticks per person; picture of a crowd; felt-tip pens; brown or black paper; small pieces of cloth; a small bag

Decorate one lolly stick to be Jesus and the other to be blind Bartimaeus. Flip Bartimaeus over and make him healed. Fold in half your crowd picture so that the crowd stands up. Cut a road out of paper. Cut a small piece of material for the cloak. Take the story home with you in the bag.

Talk about the story and how Bartimaeus had faith that Jesus could heal him. Using your story pieces, who could you tell this story to?

Celebration

You will need volunteers for a narrator, Bartimaeus and Jesus, and everyone else is part of the crowd. Participants could use their megaphones, so their voices are louder during the skit.

Narrator	Jesus travelled to many different places to talk about and share God's love with others. One day, Jesus was walking along a road to Jericho. Crowds of people lined up along the road. There was also a blind man, named Bartimaeus, sitting with the crowd begging for food and money. When Bartimaeus heard that Jesus was coming, he began to shout as loud as he could, 'Jesus, help me!'
Bartimaeus	Jesus, help me!
Narrator	The crowd began to tell Bartimaeus to be quiet. Some of them even shushed him.
Crowd	Be quiet! Shhhh!
Narrator	Unfortunately, during this time people in Bartimaeus' position were looked down on and treated without respect. Bartimaeus refused to be quieted and continued to shout louder, because even though he could not see, he knew that Jesus had the power to heal him. Jesus heard Bartimaeus' shouts and said, 'Bring that man to me.'
Jesus	Bring that man to me.
Narrator	Bartimaeus threw his only possession, the cloak he was wearing, aside, and the crowd helped him get to Jesus. Once Bartimaeus was in front of Jesus, Jesus asked him, 'What do you want me to do for you?'
Jesus	What do you want me to do for you?
Narrator	Bartimaeus responded, 'I want to see.'
Bartimaeus	I want to see.
Narrator	Bartimaeus was instantly healed and could see. Jesus told Bartimaeus, 'Go! Your faith has healed you!'
Jesus	Go! Your faith has healed you!
Narrator	Bartimaeus understood the power that Jesus had. He trusted that Jesus could heal him and he did. Bartimaeus getting his sight back gave him a new start in life. What an amazing God of new starts he met that day!

Prayer

In this story, the people in the crowd were calling out to Jesus as he passed by. Bartimaeus was calling for help. Tonight we are going to pray out loud by shouting (or at least asking loudly) all at the same time what we need God to help us with.

Dear loving and gracious God, we give thanks in knowing that we can come to you and ask for what we need. God, please help these people (*everyone says loudly the name of someone who needs help*). God, please help our community (*everyone says what the community needs help with*). God, please help our world to (*everyone says what they feel the world needs help with*). God, please help me (*everyone says what they need from God*). And let the people say… AMEN!

Song suggestions

'I see God in you' – Heather Price
'Praise ye the Lord (alleluia)' – author unknown, may be based on a Wesleyan hymn
'Ask, seek, knock' – Hillsong Kids

Meal suggestion

Build your own baked potato with toppings, with fruit and brownies for dessert.

10

Session material: October 2021

Go to messychurch.org.uk/getmessysep21 to download all templates at A4 size, including a session planning sheet.

If you are using these sessions for a Messy Church at home, look out for this symbol! These are activities that can easily be adapted to the home.

Bible story

1 Kings 17 (NIV, abridged)

Now Elijah the Tishbite, from Tishbe in Gilead, said to Ahab, 'As the Lord, the God of Israel, lives, whom I serve, there will be neither dew nor rain in the next few years except at my word.'

Then the word of the Lord came to Elijah: 'Leave here, turn eastward and hide in the Kerith Ravine, east of the Jordan. You will drink from the brook, and I have instructed the ravens to supply you with food there'...

Some time later the brook dried up because there had been no rain in the land. Then the word of the Lord came to him: 'Go at once to Zarephath in the region of Sidon and stay there. I have instructed a widow there to supply you with food.' So he went to Zarephath. When he came to the town gate, a widow was there gathering sticks. He called to her and asked, 'Would you bring me a little water in a jar so I may have a drink?' As she was going to get it, he called, 'And bring me, please, a piece of bread.'

'As surely as the Lord your God lives,' she replied, 'I don't have any bread – only a handful of flour in a jar and a little olive oil in a jug. I am gathering a few sticks to take home and make a meal for myself and my son, that we may eat it – and die.'

Elijah said to her, 'Don't be afraid. Go home and do as you have said. But first make a small loaf of bread for me from what you have and bring it to me, and then make something for yourself and your son. For this is what the Lord, the God of Israel, says: "The jar of flour will not be used up and the jug of oil will not run dry until the day the Lord sends rain on the land"'...

Some time later the son of the woman who owned the house became ill. He grew worse and worse, and finally stopped breathing. She said to Elijah, 'What do you have against me, man of God? Did you come to remind me of my sin and kill my son?'

'Give me your son,' Elijah replied. He took him from her arms, carried him to the upper room where he was staying, and laid him on his bed. Then he cried out to the Lord, 'Lord my God, have you brought tragedy even on this widow I am staying with, by causing her son to die?' Then he stretched himself out on the boy three times and cried out to the Lord, 'Lord my God, let this boy's life return to him!'

The Lord heard Elijah's cry, and the boy's life returned to him, and he lived.

Pointers

In the New Testament we are told that Elijah was a person just like us, and yet God used him as a remarkable prophet and man of prayer. He was also like us in that he was often scared, at least once was very depressed and at times felt very alone.

Today's story begins on a spiritual high: in obedience to God, Elijah confronts the ungodly rule of King Ahab and warns him of a drought that might bring him to his senses. However, this public stand exposes Elijah to danger and so he has to go into hiding.

In today's story we find him 'locked down' beside a brook, east of the river Jordan; and then later he finds refuge outside Israel, staying with a foreigner. In each of these uncomfortable and unwelcome places, God is with him, both providing for his needs and also blessing those who look after him.

Fear and loneliness are part of our experience of life, and God cares about both. God's perfect love can cast out our fear and keep us safe when, like Elijah, our freedom is threatened, our hopes are dashed or we fear for our lives.

#discipleship: team

Messy health check

Burnout is a real problem. Do any of your team need a sabbatical?

Messy team theme

- Do you know what fears and worries are troubling your Messy Church families at this time?
- What personal stories can you share about God being with you when you were scared, lonely or far from home?
- Around Halloween this month, there can be confused ideas that raise fears for some families. How might this story relate to feelings surrounding this 'festival'?

How does this session help people grow in Christ?

Elijah's story is one with which we can hugely identify. He is certainly a faithful and obedient servant of God, but at the same time we find him fearing for the future, in need of help from outsiders and engaged in desperate prayer when

Alone and scared by Martyn Payne

things seem to go wrong. It's important that we offer our Messy Church families a rounded picture of the life of faith. Yes, there are answered prayers, moments of intimacy with God and miraculous transformations, but there is also the everyday routine of staying faithful when things don't work out quickly, plans get changed and there are long periods of just waiting for the next thing God has for us. Elijah's story, which in this chapter covers a three-year period in his life, raises all these important issues. God's work in our lives may have its highlights, but in the end it's the long haul that matters.

#discipleship: families

Mealtime card
- Can you tell everyone about a time when you were scared and how you got through it?
- Have you ever had to receive help from someone you didn't know?
- Have you ever experienced God's special help when you were in need?

Take-home idea
In the story, the ravens were sent to look after Elijah when he was in hiding. However, it's usually people who look after birds when water and food are scarce. As a way to remember the story, set up a bird-feeding station in your garden, or on your balcony, with water and seeds. There are ideas for bird feeders online. Keep a record of what birds come to your feeding station. Just as you care for the birds, God cares for your family.

Question to start and end the session
So… how does God help us when we get scared?

#discipleship: extra

Elijah showed great courage in speaking out against the ungodly regime of King Ahab. He was also clearly a man of prayer. Christians today are called, as part of their discipleship, to stand up for what is right, call out injustice and pray about the big issues of our world, not just for our own needs.

As a Messy Church family, or individually in your homes, spend some time looking through the newspapers or news online together and identifying key issues about which you as a family can pray. As you pray, ask God what you might be able to do to be brave and make a difference for good with God in this world, as Elijah did.

Social action
Elijah was very grateful for God's provision when he was in hiding from King Ahab. Sadly, there are many people on the run today from unjust regimes and dangerous situations in other countries. Can your household – or you could do this with another household – find out about any refugee projects that exist in your area? Can you investigate ways in which you can help? For example, raising money or collecting furniture or food for those in need, just as Elijah was looked after by the widow's family in his need.

Activities

1. Rain stick

You will need: cardboard tubes; aluminium foil; decorative paper; scissors; masking tape; pasta and/or rice; sticky decorative ribbon and felt-tip pens

Scrunch the foil into a long snake and twist it helter-skelter style. Put this inside your cardboard tube. Seal one end of the tube with masking tape. Pour in the pasta/rice. Seal the other end with tape. Decorate your rain stick with colourful paper or felt-tip pens. As you tip your rain stick, hear the rain fall, but then stop the rain by holding the tube horizontally.

Talk about how Elijah had told King Ahab that the rain would stop for three years. Talk about what bravery that took and what faith Elijah had in God's words.

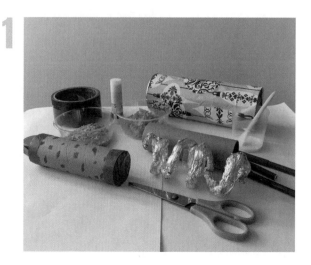

Session material: October 2021

2. Make-it-rain experiment

You will need: glass jars; hot water in a vacuum flask (to be looked after and poured by an adult); some ice cubes or ice packs; plates

Pour hot water into a clear jar to a depth of 5 cm. Put a plate on top of the jar and wait for a few moments before putting ice cubes or the ice packs on to the plate. Watch rain in the form of condensation forming on the insides of the jar, as warm air rises hitting cold air and creating 'rain'.

Talk about how God created our earth's unique climate.

3. Fed and watered

You will need: string; raven outlines (download online); cocktail sausages; pieces of bread; a full water jug; some tarpaulin to protect the floor

Make copies of the raven templates and use string to tie pieces of cocktail sausages or bread to the cut-out birds. Set up a line high above your activity area and tie the birds on to this. The challenge is to eat the meat and the bread from the birds without using your hands. Follow this by pouring water from your jug into the hands of those who take part so they can drink from cupped hands, as Elijah did from the brook.

Talk about whether Elijah was scared of the ravens that fed him. I wonder why God chose these particular birds.

4. Pick-up sticks

You will need: a set/sets of commercially available pick-up sticks, or homemade sets using bamboo skewers with the sharp ends removed

Hold the sticks bunched together vertically and then let them fall. The idea is for each player to recover one stick at a time without disturbing the others. Maybe you can turn this into a pick-up sticks competition?

Talk about how the widow at Zarephath was picking up sticks to make a fire for what she thought would be her last meal.

5. Kerith to Zarephath

You will need: items for an obstacle course – see below

After the brook dried up, Elijah was told by God to go to Sidon. This was where Ahab's wife came from, so he must've been very scared; but God knew best. The long journey must have been risky. Set up a small obstacle course for your 'Elijahs' to negotiate, including: something to climb over; something to crawl under; something to squeeze through; something to put on as a disguise and then take off. Also include some running on the spot; some creeping on tiptoes; some standing still for a minute, disguised as a tree! Make this a fun experience of what must have been a scary journey.

Talk about how Elijah felt on this journey. How would you have felt?

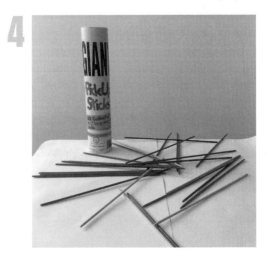

@MessyChurchBRF

Alone and scared by Martyn Payne

6. Olive oil bread

You will need: flour; baking powder; olive oil; salt; warm water; a small non-stick frying pan; a mixing bowl; a small camping gas burner

To make four small rolls, create dough from 140 g flour, 1 tsp baking powder, 2 tsp olive oil, ½ tsp salt and 120 ml of warm water. Knead the mixture and then separate it into four small rolls. Cook for five minutes in the pan which has been lightly coated with oil.

Talk about how the olive oil and flour owned by the widow did not run out while Elijah was staying with her.

7. Fill with life

You will need: round balloons; long balloons; a balloon pump; a pair of shorts; string; scissors; a marker pen

God, who cared for Elijah, looked after the widow, even when her son was fatally ill. Blow up a small round balloon and a bigger round balloon. Attach these with string as the head and body of the child. Blow up four long balloons as arms and legs, each attached by lengths of string to wrap around the neck of the balloon child. Put on some child's shorts and draw on a face.

Talk about how God's breath – God's Spirit – brought the child back to life.

8. High-level prayer

You will need: small rectangles of cardboard; pens; a high ledge

Using the cardboard rectangles to represent small stretchers, draw the outline of a person and write on each the name of someone you know who is unwell. Then lift this up with both hands and place it on a high ledge nearby, just as Elijah took the boy to his upstairs room. Use these prayer stretchers as part of your prayers in the celebration.

Talk about the different ways we can pray for those who are unwell. Christians sometimes anoint people with oil as a picture of the Holy Spirit being at work to heal. Lifting people up in your hands (in your imagination) is another way.

9. The guest room

You will need: building materials, such as Lego, Duplo or homemade Play-Doh; some small Lego bases or equivalent; fabric or felt; long matchsticks with heads removed; sticky tack

Most village homes in those days had flat roofs, and it is very probable that Elijah's makeshift room was a tent on that roof. Build a simple one-storey house with your building materials and create a flat roof. On that roof construct Elijah's room from an A-frame of sticks stuck together and some fabric.

Talk about how kind the widow was to welcome Elijah. God cares about our homes and all that happens there.

Session material: October 2021

10. Just enough

You will need: pipettes: some oil; a bowl; a phone timer

Elijah was on the run and in hiding for three years, waiting for God to tell him what to do next. In that time, the oil never ran out. Fill a small container with a measured amount of oil. The challenge is to pipette it all (a tiny drop at a time) into a second bowl in three minutes exactly, to represent the three years in the story. (You could change the time if people have shorter attention spans.)

Talk about how God promises to provide us with enough of what we need to do whatever God asks of us.

Celebration

For the story, you will need a set of brightly coloured pieces of card or paper – as many colours as you can find!

Today's story is a colourful one! I don't mean that the people wore colourful clothes (though perhaps they did); or that the countryside and places were especially colourful (though I'm sure they were); or that the sky turned different colours with different sorts of weather (though that might have happened). I mean people's moods were colourful, especially Elijah's!

The Bible says that Elijah was just like you and me and, let's face it, we all go through different feelings and moods, even in one day. We sometimes link our moods to colours. I wonder what moods or feelings you link these colours to.

Show some of the different colours. For example, red might be linked to being angry, blue to feeling sad, white to feeling scared or a bright cheerful orange to feeling happy. There are no set rules for what colour equals what mood.

We are going to use colours to help tell today's story of Elijah.

Elijah was someone who listened to God. He came close to God in prayer and God came close to him. We call him a prophet. That doesn't mean, though, that he was always perfect and full of faith. God works with all sorts of people, who can be a mixture of feelings, just like you and me.

One day Elijah felt strong in faith. (Which colour shall we choose for strong faith?) He went to King Ahab, who was a terrible king, and challenged him to change his lifestyle. To show that God was serious, Elijah said there would be no rain for three years.

Ahab was furious. (Which colour shall we choose for furious?) He put out an arrest warrant for Elijah.

Elijah was scared. (Which colour shall we choose for scared?) He ran far away to the east and hid in a valley by a stream. Elijah became very depressed. (Which colour shall we choose for depressed?) Had God given up on him?

But God looked after Elijah and sent some ravens – which must've been frightening for Elijah. (Which colour shall we choose for fear?) But then he saw they had some food for him – some meat and bread. Elijah was very thankful. (Which colour shall we choose for feeling thankful?) But after a while, because there was no rain, the stream dried up. Elijah got very worried. (Which colour shall we choose for worry?)

God told him to go far north into enemy territory. Now Elijah was confused. (Which colour shall we choose for confused?) But God had arranged for someone to look after him. At the city gates, he met a widow who was very sad. (Which colour shall we choose for sad?) She'd not only lost her husband, but now there was also no food left for her and her son.

Elijah felt strong and trusted in God. (Which colour did we choose for strong faith?. He asked for some water and bread. She had water but only enough to make bread for herself and

Alone and scared by Martyn Payne

her son. The lady was frightened. (Which colour did we choose for fear?) Elijah said that God would provide enough flour and oil for bread for all three and God did! In fact their supplies never ran out for three years. Everyone was amazed. (Which colour shall we choose for amazed?)

During Elijah's stay, however, the widow's son got very ill and died. Everyone was so sad. (Which colour did we choose for sad?) Elijah was angry with God and so was the widow. (Which colour did we choose for angry?) Elijah prayed for help. (Which colour shall we choose for being prayerful?) God gave him an idea of what to do. He took the boy and prayed over him and he came back to life.

Everyone was thrilled. (Which colour shall we choose for thrilled?) The widow was sure that God was with Elijah and that God loved them all. (Which colour shall we choose for feeling loved?)

God is with us whatever mood we are in! God does not give up on us because we are moody. And God uses us with all our mood swings, because he loves – every one of us – however we are feeling.

Prayer

Use some of the colours as a framework for your praying together. For example:

Blue – Let's bring our sadness to God, about others and about ourselves, and say sorry…

Dark grey – Let's bring our worries to God and ask for God's peace…

Brown (link this to the brown cardboard 'stretchers' used in the prayer activity) – Let's bring those who are unwell to God and ask for his help…

A variety of colours like a rainbow – Let's bring our celebrations to God and say thank you…

Song suggestions

'We your children' – Fischy Music (Bring it all to me)
'You are a star' – Fischy Music (Build up)
'God who made the earth (… will care for me)' – Junior Praise
'God cares for you' – John Hardwick
'Every step' – Nick and Becky Drake
'God's people aren't super brave superheroes' – John Hardwick

Meal suggestion

Why not have a meal that involves mini sausages and croutons to remind you of the food that the ravens brought? Include some small bread rolls too, just like the ones that the widow made.

Session material: November 2021

Go to **messychurch.org.uk/getmessysep21** to download all templates at A4 size, including a session planning sheet.

If you are using these sessions for a Messy Church at home, look out for this symbol! These are activities that can easily be adapted to the home.

Bible story

Acts 9:36–43 (GNT)

In Joppa there was a woman named Tabitha, who was a believer. (Her name in Greek is Dorcas, meaning 'a deer.') She spent all her time doing good and helping the poor. At that time she got sick and died. Her body was washed and laid in a room upstairs. Joppa was not very far from Lydda, and when the believers in Joppa heard that Peter was in Lydda, they sent two men to him with the message, 'Please hurry and come to us.' So Peter got ready and went with them. When he arrived, he was taken to the room upstairs, where all the widows crowded around him, crying and showing him all the shirts and coats that Dorcas had made while she was alive. Peter put them all out of the room, and knelt down and prayed; then he turned to the body and said, 'Tabitha, get up!' She opened her eyes, and when she saw Peter, she sat up. Peter reached over and helped her get up. Then he called all the believers, including the widows, and presented her alive to them. The news about this spread all over Joppa, and many people believed in the Lord. Peter stayed on in Joppa for many days with a tanner of leather named Simon.

Pointers

Have you ever 'put your foot in your mouth' and said something you really shouldn't have? Did you notice that in this story, we do not hear of anything that Tabitha *said*, just what she *did*. Will we be remembered for our actions and not our words? I do hope so!

There is a lot about the story that we must work out for ourselves. It does not say if Tabitha was young or old, rich or poor, married or a widow. I love stories like this, ones that you must study and think about, just like the parables that Jesus told.

Tabitha had an 'upper room' which she was laid out in, so she may well have been rich. She was surrounded by widows, so could have been a widow herself. Her name meant 'gazelle' (or 'deer'), so she might have been slim and beautiful. Have

you noticed how the Bible hardly every comments on what someone looks like, not even Jesus himself? Her beauty was not important; it was her deeds that shone out.

Did you know that Tabitha was the only woman in the New Testament specifically named as a *disciple*? What a badge of honour! Yet she did not part the Red Sea like Moses, build an ark like Noah, cure cancer or eradicate world hunger; she sewed clothes. When we play down our simple acts of kindness, we should remember Tabitha!

#discipleship: team

Messy health check

Does anyone come to mind who would benefit from joining your friendly team?

Messy team theme

- Do your actions speak louder than your words?
- How often do you intentionally copy Jesus' actions?
- How can you help other people, even in small ways, knowing that God sees this and is pleased?

How does this session help people grow in Christ?

In raising Tabitha, Peter copied Jesus almost exactly. Jesus raised a little girl from the dead in Mark 5:38–43. He was presented with a crowd of crying mourners, put them out of the room and, with Peter watching, took her hand and said, 'Talitha, koum!', which means, 'Little girl, I tell you to get up!' Peter changed just one letter and said, 'Tabitha, koum!'

As Christians, that is exactly what we are called to do – to copy Jesus in order to become more like him. In this session, we will make gifts for others, think about our own selfishness and consider what gifts God has given us and how we might use them to copy Jesus and help others. In 1 Peter 4:10, Peter himself sums up the importance of serving: 'Each one should use whatever gift he has received to serve others.'

#discipleship: families

Mealtime card

- Tabitha could sew. What are your gifts?
- How must Peter have been feeling when he said, 'Tabitha, koum'? Scared? Embarrassed? Unsure? Confident?
- Tabitha's nickname was 'Gazelle'. What would your animal nickname be?

Sew miraculous! by Sharon Sampson

Take-home idea

Why not have a big sort out and take some toys and clothes to the local charity shop or to someone you know who might need them?

Question to start and end the session

So… how do you copy Jesus and help others?

#discipleship: extra

Hold a 'Promise Auction' where people offer their skills and talents, such as mowing a lawn, pet-sitting or making a birthday cake. Give the money raised to charity.

Social action

Bake a cake for a lonely neighbour. Send a letter or postcard to let someone know you are thinking of them. Leave a bunch of flowers on someone's doorstep.

Activities

1. Sugar scrub

You will need: sugar; jam jars; oil (coconut, olive, etc.); lemon juice; scraps of material; scissors; rubber bands; card labels; pens; spoons

Make an exfoliating sugar scrub as a gift for someone. Use small jam jars to save materials. Cut out circles of material to cover the lids, securing with rubber bands. Add a label as a finishing touch.

Talk about how Tabitha was the only woman in the Bible to be named as a 'disciple', which was quite an honour – yet she did not cure cancer or solve world poverty; she made clothes for the poor. In the same way, your simple act of giving this gift to someone is really important to God. Colossians 3:23 says: 'Whatever you do, work at it with all your heart, as though you were working for the Lord and not for people.'

2. Stress ball

You will need: balloons (biodegradable if possible); wool; marker pens; empty water bottles; flour or sand; funnel

Using the funnel, fill the water bottle with flour or sand. Blow up the balloon, twist the neck and then carefully place the balloon mouth over the bottle. Tip it up and transfer the flour to the balloon. Carefully release all the air. Tie a knot in the balloon. Loop some wool around your fingers, then tie it in the middle and then tie it to the balloon. Cut through the ends of the loops of wool. Clean it off, then draw a silly face on it.

Talk about how we can all get stressed out, so these balls will make a great gift. Why not give it to someone and use it as an opener to help them chat about what is worrying them?

3. Basket weaving

You will need: paper plates; scissors; a hole punch; old T-shirts

Cut 10 cm down from the edge of the plate. Repeat 15 more times, all the way around. Make each cut wider so that there is room for the material. Cut 1 cm strips of T-shirt material and stretch them out. Weave them in and out of the paper plate, pulling up the sides as you go, to get a basket shape. Punch a hole at the top of each strip, then finish it off by threading through the holes. Add a fabric handle if you wish.

Talk about how Tabitha made clothes to give to the poor, possibly because Jesus said in Matthew 25:40, 'I tell you, whenever you did this for one of the least important of these followers of mine, you did it for me!' She may well have weaved her own cloth or made baskets to give away. Why not give this as a gift to someone? What could you put inside?

Session material: November 2021

4. Tapestry prayer station

You will need: a loom made of some chicken wire attached to an old picture frame, or string wound tightly around a frame; strips of material of different colours, including black; printout of 'My life is but a weaving', a poem attributed to Corrie ten Boom, or another poem

Read the poem, then weave some material into the group tapestry. Think and pray about how you can trust God with the highs and lows of life, as only he can see the big picture.

Talk about how life is a tapestry of colours, bright and dark. We don't always know why the dark threads are needed, but God does. At the end of our lives, we will understand too.

5. T-shirt apron

You will need: lots of large old T-shirts; sewing scissors

Cut off the sleeves. Leaving the collar intact, cut off the top half of the back of the T-shirt. Then, leaving a 5 cm strip across the back, cut off the bottom half of the back of the T-shirt. Cut the 5 cm strip in half lengthways, leaving one end attached on the right and one end attached on the left. These will be your apron ties. Pull them tight to make them more string-like.

3

4

Talk about how Tabitha made clothes for the poor. She may well have made new clothes out of old, just like you are doing. This is a great way to help the planet by reducing waste.

6. Skilful cookies

You will need: butter; sugar; eggs; dried fruit (dates, apricots, sultanas, etc.); desiccated coconut; chocolate chips; oats; plain flour; vanilla extract; mixing bowls; wooden spoons; measuring spoons; baking trays lined with baking paper; an oven; paper gift bags (optional)

Cream a 3 cm x 3 cm cube of butter, 1 tbsp sugar and a few drops of vanilla essence. Add ½ beaten egg and beat together until light and fluffy. Add 1 cup of the fruit, chocolate and coconut and 1 cup of oats, then 1 tbsp flour. Mix using your hands and form into balls. Flatten and place on a lined baking tray (write names on baking paper next to the biscuits). Cook for 20 minutes at 180ºC. Place in paper gift bags if possible.

Talk about how Tabitha's skill was sewing and she used that to help others. What is your skill? Is it cooking? Who could you cheer up by giving these biscuits to?

7. Washing games

You will need: pegs; a scoreboard; a washing line; clothes

How many pegs can you hold in one hand without dropping them? How fast can you peg out all the washing? Prizes per age group.

5

Sew miraculous! by Sharon Sampson

Talk about how our hands are a gift from God. No matter how big or small our hands are, we can still use them to help others. In the game speed was important, but often to help others, we need to slow down and look around us, to see who needs our help. Do you know someone who needs your help? Maybe even someone less mobile than yourself who would like help putting out their washing!

8. Mannequin dress-up

You will need: a mannequin (or clothes rack or volunteer); bits of material; safety pins; clips; pegs

As a group, dress up the mannequin, giving them an amazing outfit.

Talk about how our story today is about Tabitha, who made clothes for others.

6

7

9. Fashion designer

You will need: rectangular white paper; pens; scissors; cocktail sticks; sticky tape; pretty paper

Make a little booklet out of the paper by folding it in half three times, then cutting a thin slit in the middle. Make a head out of paper and a cocktail stick, and stick it inside the booklet. Design four outfits for your little person to wear.

Talk about when Tabitha made clothes for others, do you think she thought about each person as she made them, pouring love into each item?

10. Dress-up chocolate

You will need: chocolate bars; a hat; a scarf; gloves; dice; knives and forks

A group game to play together, taking turns to throw the dice. If you get a six, put on the clothes before eating the chocolate with a knife and fork. Meanwhile, everyone else keeps rolling; if someone else throws a six, they interrupt and take over.

Talk about how in this game, we very quickly become selfish, as we want the chocolate. Did everyone have a fair share? Jesus wants us to think about others too, to notice when people don't have enough and need our help, just like Tabitha.

Celebration

Start with a game of sleeping lions – get everyone to lie on the floor and be very still. If anyone moves, they are out. Keep playing until you get a winner or have a time limit.

Our story today is about someone who had died and whose body was laid out in a room, very still, just like you tried to be. But she wasn't pretending, she was really dead.

Alternatively, play a simple game of 'Simon Says', because in this story Peter copied what he saw Jesus doing.

To make the story fun and to emphasise the similarity between the stories of Jesus raising a little girl and Peter raising Tabitha, tell both stories at the same time! You could have the storytellers acting the parts of the messengers and get volunteers or helpers to play the parts of Jesus, Peter, a little girl and Tabitha.

Narrator 1 Shall I tell the story?

Narrator 2 Yes please.

Narrator 1 One day, a man came to Jesus, fell at his feet and begged him…

Session material: November 2021
Sew miraculous! by Sharon Sampson

Narrator 2 No! That's not the story!

Narrator 1 What do you mean? I thought we were telling the story of Jesus raising the little girl.

Narrator 2 No! The story of Peter raising Tabitha.

Narrator 1 Oh! Can't I tell my story?

Narrator 2 I'm sorry. But we need to tell the Tabitha story.

Narrator 1 (*sulking*) But I've spent ages preparing it.

Narrator 2 Oh, dear. We haven't got long enough to tell both stories

Narrator 1 Well, can we tell them both at the same time?

Narrator 2 Umm. Okay. I suppose we can try.

We need volunteers for Peter and Jesus. (*Position Peter and Narrator 2 on one side, and Jesus and Narrator 1 on the other. Get two 'dead' volunteers to lay down in the middle.*)

Narrator 1 One day, a man came to **Jesus**, fell at his feet and begged him, '**My daughter** is dying. Please come and heal her.'

Narrator 2 One day, a man came to **Peter**, fell at his feet and begged him, '**Tabitha** has died, please come at once and help her.'

Narrator 1 So **Jesus** went with him (*lead Jesus to the little girl*).

Narrator 2 So **Peter** went with him (*lead Peter to Tabitha*).

Narrator 1 When **Jesus** arrived at the house, the girl was already dead, and a crowd of people were there crying. I said, the crowd were crying!

Narrator 2 When **Peter** arrived at the house, a crowd of widows were there crying.

Narrator 1 **Jesus** made the crowd stay outside and went into the **little girl's** room.

Narrator 2 **Peter** made the crowd stay outside and went into **Tabitha's** room.

Narrator 1 **Jesus** took her by the hand and said, '**Talitha, koum**', which means, 'Little girl, I say to you, get up.'

Narrator 2 **Peter** turned to the dead woman and said, '**Tabitha, koum**', which means, 'Tabitha, I say to you, get up.'

Narrator 1 Immediately the **little girl** stood up and began walking around.

Narrator 2 **Tabitha** opened her eyes and sat up and Peter took her hand and helped her to her feet.

It's well-known that Jesus raised Lazarus, who had been dead for several days, but Jesus also raised a 12-year-old girl. When he did it, Peter was a witness, in the room with him. So, sometime later, when Peter was asked to raise Tabitha from death, he had the confidence to follow in Jesus' footsteps, copying almost exactly what he did and bringing Tabitha back to life.

Our story today was about two quite ordinary people. Peter was a fisherman and Tabitha sewed clothes for the poor. They did not eradicate world hunger or discover a cure for cancer. In the same way, we don't have to do something that's worthy of winning a Nobel Prize for God to take note of what we have done. What are our gifts and talents? Sewing? Encouraging? Cooking? Organising? Leadership? Fixing things? Whatever they are, use those gifts and talents to serve others, and God will be smiling in heaven!

Prayer

Let's play chat and catch – we will **chat** to God and try to **catch** what he is saying to us. Sometimes God can talk to us through music we play or things we read, and sometimes it can be through pictures or thoughts that appear in our heads. Let's close our eyes to help us listen.

Make a thumbs-up sign – Tell God which activity you enjoyed the most today. (*Pause.*) Thank you, Lord, for all the fun we have had at Messy Church today. Thank you for all the people that use their time and talents to put it all together for us.

Hold your palms out like you are accepting a present – Ask God to show you the gift he gave you that he wants you to use to help others. (*Pause.*) Thank you, Lord for all the talents you have given us. As we go about our daily lives this coming week, remind us to copy Jesus and to use those talents to help others.

Thank you, Lord, for your Son Jesus, who gives us an amazing example to try to follow. Thank you that we can read all about him in the Bible. Thank you that, just as Tabitha had a new life after death, we too can look forward to a new life in heaven with you. Amen

Song suggestions

'Be bold, be strong' – Morris Chapman
'Make a difference' – Out of the Ark
'When I needed a neighbour' – Sydney Carter

Meal suggestion

As we have been thinking about Tabitha helping the poor, you could make a big sign, 'Soup Kitchen', and offer two or three flavours of soup, served out of slow cookers, along with bread rolls.

Session material: December 2021
The birth of Jesus by Mark and Jane Hird-Rutter

Go to **messychurch.org.uk/getmessysep21** to download all templates at A4 size, including a session planning sheet.

If you are using these sessions for a Messy Church at home, look out for this symbol! These are activities that can easily be adapted to the home.

Pointers

In our Messy Church we will focus on the following:

- Mary and Joseph were obedient to God.
- Mary pondered what she was told and saw.
- It was made clear that Jesus was the Saviour, the Messiah and the Son of God.
- Mary and Joseph were thoughtful and dedicated parents.

Bible story

Luke 2 (NIV, abridged)

Caesar Augustus issued a decree that a census should be taken of the entire Roman world… And everyone went to their own town to register.

So Joseph also went up from the town of Nazareth in Galilee to Judea, to Bethlehem…. He went there to register with Mary, who was pledged to be married to him and was expecting a child. While they were there, the time came for the baby to be born, and she gave birth to her firstborn, a son. She wrapped him in cloths and placed him in a manger…

And there were shepherds living out in the fields near by, keeping watch over their flocks at night. An angel of the Lord appeared to them, and the glory of the Lord shone around them, and they were terrified. But the angel said to them, 'Do not be afraid. I bring you good news that will cause great joy for all the people. Today in the town of David a Saviour has been born to you; he is the Messiah, the Lord…'

Suddenly a great company of the heavenly host appeared with the angel, praising God and saying, 'Glory to God in the highest heaven, and on earth peace to those on whom his favour rests.'

When the angels had left them and gone into heaven, the shepherds said to one another, 'Let's go to Bethlehem and see this thing that has happened, which the Lord has told us about.'

So they hurried off and found Mary and Joseph, and the baby, who was lying in the manger. When they had seen him, they spread the word concerning what had been told them about this child, and all who heard it were amazed at what the shepherds said to them. But Mary treasured up all these things and pondered them in her heart. The shepherds returned, glorifying and praising God for all the things they had heard and seen, which were just as they had been told.

#discipleship: team

Messy health check

In a busy month, is there anyone on the team who needs particular prayer?

Messy team theme

- Christmas is a time for reflection. How do you take time to ponder the real reason for Christmas?
- In this hectic time during Christmas, how do you find peace?
- What makes Christmas special for you?

How does this session help people grow in Christ?

Mary grew in faith as she pondered what she saw and heard from God. To ponder is to think carefully and reflect before acting. As a Messy Church community, the act of pondering will help us learn about ourselves and grow closer to Christ.

#discipleship: families

Mealtime card

- How does your family celebrate the birth of Christ?
- Christmas is often overwhelmed with commercialism. What does your family do that is special for Christmas in a Christian sense?

Take-home idea

Show the manger scene (activity 7) to some friends and show them how to make one for themselves. Talk about the people in the scene and what they did in the Christmas story.

Question to start and end the session

So… how do you help to bring 'peace on earth' at this time of year?

Session material: December 2021

#discipleship: extra

The story of Jesus' birth is a message of peace for the world. How could you spread peace throughout your neighbourhood? Try singing Christmas carols. How about working at a food bank or helping people with shopping or chores?

Social action

This is a great time of year to reduce, reuse and recycle. Try wrapping presents in reusable cloth bags or giving experiences instead of physical presents. Give 'gifts of hope': buy a goat, or school supplies for someone in a developing country.

Activities

1. Cloth gift bag

You will need: small cloth craft bags; a variety of paint and brushes, or cloth marker pens

Paint a Christmas design on the cloth bag. Put a present in the bag and give it to someone special in your life for a Christmas present.

Talk about how important it is for the planet when we are careful and recycle. Often paper wrap is not recycled.

2. Helping our environment and others

You will need: leftover wrapping paper; old Christmas cards; old ribbon; glue; scissors; poster board; felt-tip pens

Design a poster about how to help save our environment, reusing the old material on the table.

Talk about ways to help the environment at this time of year.

3. Love gift box

You will need: small jewellery boxes; paper; pens; pencil crayons; wrapping paper; ribbon

On the paper, write a note to the recipient of your box. Tell them how much you love them and how special they are to you. Decorate the note, then fold it and put it into the box. Wrap the box in the paper and tie the ribbon around it.

Talk about how important it is to tell people how much you care for them.

4. Taking a census

You will need: a census spreadsheet to count people (download online); pencils; pens; pins; a large world map

Set up a census table and have each participant visit the table through the activity time. Enter data for each person. (The supplied spreadsheet will count the number of people and determine the minimum and maximum age.) Alter the spreadsheet to collect other information, e.g. how many different countries are represented in your Messy Church. Place a pin on the map to show where everyone was born. (People's personal information is protected in many countries. Once the Messy Church is completed, it may be necessary or advisable to delete the data.)

The birth of Jesus by Mark and Jane Hird-Rutter

Talk about why we take a census today. What is the collected data used for?

5. Christmas photo shoot

You will need: a backdrop Bethlehem stable scene, including a manger with a baby Jesus doll; Christmas costumes; a camera; a printer for printing the photos

Dress up as Christmas figures and have your picture taken with Jesus. Use the picture to make a Christmas card if desired.

Talk about why we go and visit Santa at Christmas. What happened in the Bethlehem stable?

6. Shepherd's table

You will need: a blanket; various food from the Middle East: bread, grapes, olives, cheese, dried fruits, sliced meat, etc.

Set up a blanket and picnic to find out what the shepherds might have eaten for their dinner when they met the angel.

Talk about what it must have been like to be a shepherd in the time of Jesus. What would it be like at night in the hills with the sheep? What did they eat while they tended their flocks by night?

7. Manger scene

You will need: wide lolly sticks; card; paint; paintbrushes; glue; pipe cleaners; ribbon

Using the card base and lolly sticks, create a small stable with a manger. Paint the figures and the manger. Wrap baby Jesus in the ribbon and give the angel a pipe-cleaner halo. Glue the scene together.

Talk about what it would have been like in the olden days to stay in a stable.

8. Journey to Bethlehem

You will need: a large piece of cardboard for the map; paint; markers; coloured paper; a set of nativity figures; extra animals, such as a donkey, a camel and sheep; wooden blocks; Lego or homemade buildings

Create a large table-sized map of the area from Nazareth to Bethlem using paint and coloured cardboard (see photo for inspiration). Draw roads and towns on the way. The one shown in the picture had homemade buildings and gates, but you could use wooden blocks or Lego, to create: the stable; Herod's palace; the temple; an inn; and sheep pens.

Work as a group and have each person choose a figure from the nativity set of different Bible characters and re-enact the journey from Nazareth to Bethlehem. Use the donkey, Mary and Joseph and interact with the innkeeper, shepherds, angels and wise men.

Talk about what it would be like for Mary to walk or ride a donkey so far, carrying an unborn child. Why did God choose a stable?

5

6

7

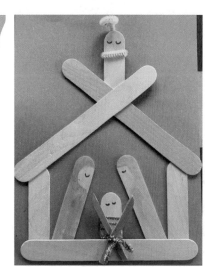

Session material: December 2021

9. Tangram Christmas story

You will need: tangrams; designs to show shapes of people from the Christmas story (download online); backing paper with the shapes of the characters

Make the Tangram shapes following the designs in the template to show the characters in the Christmas story.

Talk about how many of the shapes you were able to make. Which ones did you like best?

10. Star conjunction

You will need: a tablet or computer with star planetarium app (e.g. Stellarium: free and runs on Linux, Windows and Mac OS; Sky Safari: $16 iOS, Android, MacOS)

Run the star app and go back in time to 17 June, 2 BC. Set your position to Bethlehem. Locate Jupiter and Venus. They should be very close. When two planets are close like this, it is called a conjunction. At what time of day are they the closest? How far apart are they at their closest?

If you're struggling, you could use this video instead: **youtu.be/BfQm9YTI5VU**

Talk about how, during this conjunction, the two planets would have been so close that they would appear to be one object. Is it possible to see Jupiter or Venus in the daytime? With their combined brightness, they would have been dazzling at night. What do you think astronomers or astrologers of the time would think if the two brightest objects, after the sun and moon, came together to form one?

Celebration

Use a reporter to interview participants about the events happening in the Bible reading. This might also be possible as a puppet show or with teen actors in a play. Ask the audience to ponder carefully what they hear from the people who are interviewed.

Reporter This is [Reporter's name] with *The Bethlehem Herald*. There seems to be a lot of excitement in the town square today. There are sheep running all over the place and what looks like shepherds running around and all excited. I'll try to get an interview with one of them. Excuse me, sir, can you tell us what's going on?

Shepherd Wow, where do I start? We were tending our sheep in the hills over there and suddenly an angel appeared to us.

Reporter How did you know it was an angel?

Shepherd Well, he told me he was an angel! Then there were his blazing white robes and his shining face, and the wings were a giveaway.

Reporter So, what did he tell you?

Shepherd Well, to tell you the truth we were very frightened. He said, 'Do not fear, for I bring you good news of great joy.' We felt a bit better and calmed down. Then he continued. 'For on this day in the city of David a Saviour is born, he is the Messiah. This will be a sign to you: You will find a baby wrapped in cloths and lying in a manger.' Then the whole sky was filled by angels all singing, 'Glory to God in the highest and on earth peace to all.'

Reporter In a manger? Why would a baby be in a manger?

Shepherd We thought that, too. But when you think about it, the hotels and hostels were all full. We dashed into town and soon found there was a young couple who had taken refuge in a cave. There was the baby, a boy wrapped in swaddling clothes. He is the Messiah and that's why we are all excited.

The birth of Jesus by Mark and Jane Hird-Rutter

Reporter   Our news team is at the inn in Bethlehem. First, we have here Jonathan, the innkeeper. Would you please tell us what happened yesterday?

Jonathan   Well, we are really busy because of the census. All our courtyards and private rooms are completely full. This young couple showed up. They had been all over town and could not find any other place to stay. She was pregnant, very pregnant, and she looked very tired. We have a stable in the back. It's more like a cave where we keep our animals. It's dry and relatively clean and much less crowded than our courtyard. We thought they would do better there.

Reporter   Next we have Marian, the innkeeper's wife. What did you see?

Marian   Well, I saw the young woman – she was very young and very close to giving birth. I've had experience delivering babies, so I went to see how she was doing. When I got there she was in labour. Her husband was doing his best, but I could see him saying a 'Thank you' prayer when I arrived. The mum was wonderful. She was very young but had an amazing air about her. The birth went without complications – a little boy. Once they were settled, I took a look at the three of them. The word that comes to mind to describe them was 'Grace'. We wrapped the little one in swaddling clothes and laid him in the manger. A very sweet boy.

Reporter   I've been able to get into the stable. The young couple, Mary and Joseph, have consented to answer some questions, as long as we talk in a whisper, so we don't wake the baby. Now Mary and Joseph, congratulations on the birth of your baby. Have you chosen a name yet?

Joseph   We have decided to call him Jesus.

Reporter   Mary, how did you come to be in the centre of all this excitement? I can see you're pondering the question before answering!

Mary   An angel came to me and asked me if I would be the mother of this child. This was completely unexpected; I didn't know what to do. I sat still for a while and thought of all that this would mean to me. I quietly prayed to God and asked, 'How can I do this? Will you help me, God?' When I had done this, I found I felt a great peace and warmth and I realised that this was my path. I always try to think carefully and consider things before I act. You don't always have all the answers, but often you get a feeling, especially after praying, that it's the right thing to do.

Reporter   This has been a very exciting day in the town of Bethlehem. As the day progressed, more visitors from far away arrived. With me now I have Balthazar from Arabia. How did you and your friends find your way to this stable?

Balthazar   My friends and I are all scholars from far away. We all study the stars in the sky. Have you seen the very bright one?

Reporter   Why yes, it's hard to miss. You can even see it in the daytime.

Balthazar   Indeed, you can. My friends and I have been studying this 'star' for some time. We could see for months that it was happening and the place that it was happening is in the constellation of the Lion, 'the King'. We knew that Bethlehem was the city of King David, so we came here. We could calculate the time when the star would stop in the sky and so we planned to arrive as close to that time as we could.

Reporter   How did you know all this?

Balthazar   We watch the sky very carefully and we have instruments to measure. We are called astronomers, that's what we do.

Reporter   You brought presents with you.

Balthazar   Yes, we brought gold, frankincense and myrrh. Gifts for the King of the Jews.

Reporter   An amazing day in the little town of Bethlehem. This is [Reporter's name] with *The Bethlehem Herald*, signing off. 'Peace on earth to all people!'

Prayer

Creator God, we ask that this story, the amazing birth of Jesus, will bring us all closer to understanding the wonderful gift of your Son Jesus and all that he means and stands for. Let there be peace on earth and let it begin with us. Amen

Song suggestions

'Huron carol' – Jean de Brébeuf
'The virgin Mary had a baby boy' – traditional
'Hark the herald angels sing' – traditional
'Jesus name above all names' – Naida Hearn

Meal suggestion

Curried turkey and broccoli bake (page 30 of the *Alpha Cookbook*), with tossed salad and dressing, and buns for dessert.

Messy questions

Richard and Kayla Harlow, with St Paul's, Tadley, Messy Church

In our Messy Church, we noticed that many of our members had big questions which we didn't really have time to address. This project arose from those questions. We offer our responses to these questions here. Be assured that our responses only represent our beliefs and experience of God. They are not official Messy Church creed or set of beliefs. As well as our thoughts, we offer some questions for you to discuss with the people around you and an activity to take the topic further. Some of us find our answers by talking and some by doing, so pick up whatever works for you.

Perhaps you have a question that you'd like someone to respond to. You could write it down and give it to whoever leads your Messy Church, or send it to messychurch@brf.org.uk.

God, what are your other names?

This is a really good question! Our name tells people who we are. My name is Richard. It tells you that I am probably: male, British and quite traditional (I haven't shortened it to Ricky, Rich or Dick). Kayla's name was given to her mum by a Romany (Traveller) woman. It reminds her that her mum was a friend to Travellers.

In the Hebrew Bible (the Bible that Jesus read, our Old Testament), God is known by two words: El and Yahweh. 'El' means God, so it's not really a name, just like 'God' isn't a name. The word 'Allah' is the Arabic word for God, so El and Allah and God all mean the same thing.

But not everybody understands God the same, as we saw in our first question. People may use the word 'God' as a swear word. People may blame God for the bad things that happen in the world. So what is God like? The name Yahweh tells us.

Yahweh is God's (El's) name. It means something like 'breath' or 'spirit' or 'life'. I think it tells us that God is 'giver of life'.

Jesus gave God another name: Father – 'Our Father in heaven' (Matthew 6:9). He reminds us that God gives us life (in a different way from how our mothers give us life). He tells us that God loves us (like a good father) and that God is invisible (that's what 'in heaven' means).

Jesus tells us other things about God. He describes God as a farmer (Mark 4), as a shepherd (John 10), as a gardener (John 15) and as a judge (Matthew 25), but never as a person in the sky (like Thor). The stories that Jesus tells help us to understand the 'name' or 'character' of God. We see that God nurtures life and growth (like a farmer or gardener), that God cares and protects (like a shepherd) and that God divides good from bad (like a judge).

Across the world, people have many names for God. What matters is: do these names agree with the character that we see Jesus teach and demonstrate?

Christians call Jesus 'Son of God' or 'God', because Jesus shows us the character of God (the name of God) as clearly as we could possibly see.

Think about:

Do different people call you different names? Why? What name could you call God? Why?

Read Psalm 103 (in most English Bibles the name 'Yahweh' is written 'the LORD'). What does this psalm/poem tell us about God? What does it say God is not like?

Have a go: decide what name you want to call God, a name that describes God's character. Write your own prayer to God using that name.

Order your next issue of *Get Messy!*

Get Messy! is published three times per year in January, May and September.
Available from: your local Christian bookshop
Online: **brfonline.org.uk/getmessy**
By phone: +44 (0)1865 319700
By post: complete the form below

A **group subscription** works when you receive five or more copies of *Get Messy!* delivered to a single address. To order postage-free, go to brfonline.org.uk/products/get-messy-subscription.

Print copies

SUBSCRIPTION (INCLUDES POSTAGE AND PACKING)	PRICE	QTY	TOTAL (£)
January to December 2022 one-year subscription (UK)	£18.00		
January to December 2022 one-year subscription (Europe)	£25.95		
January to December 2022 one-year subscription (Rest of world)	£29.85		
SINGLE COPIES	PRICE	QTY	TOTAL (£)
Get Messy! September–December 2021	£4.75		
Get Messy! January–April 2022	£4.75		
Postage for single copies (see right)			
Donation to BRF's Messy Church			
		Total	

Title _____ First name/initials _____ Surname _____

Address _____

_____ Postcode _____

Telephone _____ Email _____

Method of payment

☐ Cheque (made payable to BRF) ☐ MasterCard / Visa

Card no. ☐☐☐☐ ☐☐☐☐ ☐☐☐☐ ☐☐☐☐

Valid from M M Y Y Expires M M Y Y Security code* ☐☐☐
Last 3 digits on the reverse of the card

Signature _____ Date _____
ESSENTIAL IN ORDER TO PROCESS YOUR ORDER

The **Messy Church®** name and logo are registered trade marks of The Bible Reading Fellowship, a Registered Charity (233280)

Digital copies

Single-copy purchases of the *Get Messy!* magazine are intended for the sole use of the purchaser. If you would like to distribute digital copies to your Messy Church team, simply click the **Buy now** button on the product page and add the number of copies you need into the quantity box. The following discounts will be applied for multiple copies:

1–2 copies: no discount   3–4 copies: 10% discount
5–9 copies: 15% discount   10+ copies: 20% discount

For further information about purchasing digital copies and copyright information, see **brfonline.org.uk/terms**.

POSTAGE AND PACKING CHARGES			
Order value	UK	Europe	Rest of world
Under £7.00	£2.00	Available on request	Available on request
£7.00–£29.99	£3.00		
£30.00+	FREE		

General information

Delivery times within the UK are normally 15 working days. All prices are subject to the current rate of VAT. Prices are correct at the time of going to press but may change without prior notice. Offers available while stocks last.

Return this form with the appropriate payment to:
BRF, 15 The Chambers, Vineyard, Abingdon OX14 3FE
Tel. +44 (0)1865 319700   Fax +44 (0)1865 319701

To read our terms and find out about cancelling your order, please visit **brfonline.org.uk/terms**

You can pay for your annual subscription using Direct Debit. You need only give your bank details once, and the payment is made automatically every year until you cancel it. If you would like to pay by Direct Debit, please also use the form below, entering your BRF account number under 'Reference' if you know it. You are fully covered by the Direct Debit Guarantee.

Instruction to your bank or building society to pay by Direct Debit

Please fill in the whole form using a ballpoint pen and return it to:
BRF, 15 The Chambers, Vineyard, Abingdon OX14 3FE

Service User Number: 5 5 8 2 2 9

Name and full postal address of your bank or building society

To: The Manager	Bank/Building Society
Address	
	Postcode

Name(s) of account holder(s)

Branch sort code ☐☐–☐☐–☐☐

Bank/Building Society account number ☐☐☐☐☐☐☐☐

Reference number

☐☐☐☐☐☐☐

Instruction to your Bank/Building Society

Please pay The Bible Reading Fellowship Direct Debits from the account detailed in this instruction, subject to the safeguards assured by the Direct Debit Guarantee. I understand that this instruction may remain with The Bible Reading Fellowship and, if so, details will be passed electronically to my bank/building society.

Signature(s)

Banks and Building Societies may not accept Direct Debit instructions for some types of account.

✂

The Direct Debit Guarantee

- This Guarantee is offered by all banks and building societies that accept instructions to pay Direct Debits.
- If there are any changes to the amount, date or frequency of your Direct Debit, The Bible Reading Fellowship will notify you 10 working days in advance of your account being debited or as otherwise agreed. If you request The Bible Reading Fellowship to collect a payment, confirmation of the amount and date will be given to you at the time of the request.
- If an error is made in the payment of your Direct Debit, by The Bible Reading Fellowship or your bank or building society, you are entitled to a full and immediate refund of the amount paid from your bank or building society.
- If you receive a refund you are not entitled to, you must pay it back when The Bible Reading Fellowship asks you to.
- You can cancel a Direct Debit at any time by simply contacting your bank or building society. Written confirmation may be required. Please also notify us.

For more information on the discipleship islands, see the article on page 8.

Growing the church

making life Better for others

worship

Justice

togetherness

Prayer

family

Caring for the earth

Bible Stories

Prayer

meals

Generosity

Play

UK £4.75
ISBN: 9781800390447
9 781800 390447

BRF
brf.org.uk

September-December 2021   £4.75

Messy Church

getMESSY!

Messy Church
Goes Wild!

Messy
Masterclasses

Messy
memories

Messy Church
and discipleship

Includes
Messy Church
at home
ideas

Sessions in this issue

| Trusting is believing Mark 10:46–52 | Alone and scared 1 Kings 17 | Sew miraculous! Acts 9:36–43 | The birth of Jesus Luke 2 |

BRF, 15 The Chambers, Vineyard, Abingdon OX14 3FE
+44 (0)1865 319700 | enquiries@brf.org.uk
brf.org.uk

The Messy Church® name and logo are registered trade marks of
The Bible Reading Fellowship, a Registered Charity (233280)

ISBN 978 1 80039 044 7
First published 2021
10 9 8 7 6 5 4 3 2 1 0
All rights reserved
This edition © The Bible Reading Fellowship 2021

Acknowledgements

Scripture quotations marked NIV are taken from The
Holy Bible, New International Version (Anglicised
edition) copyright © 1979, 1984, 2011 by Biblica. Used
by permission of Hodder & Stoughton Publishers,
a Hachette UK company. All rights reserved. 'NIV'
is a registered trademark of Biblica. UK trademark
number 1448790. Scripture quotations marked CEV
are taken from the Contemporary English Version.
New Testament © American Bible Society 1991, 1992,
1995. Old Testament © American Bible Society 1995.
Anglicisations © British & Foreign Bible Society 1996.
Used by permission.

Editor: Olivia Warburton
Subeditor: Rachel Tranter
Designers: Rebecca J Hall and Alison Beek
Proofreader: Daniele Och
Cover photo: Messy Church Australia, photo by
Dianne Natt
Internal photos: p. 5, top right: kira auf der heide on
Unsplash, pipe cleaner fish and craft bags by Sharon
Sampson; p. 6 by Karen Markussen; p. 7, top two: by
Dianne Natt, lower: Jocelyn Czerwonka; p. 9 by Dylan
Heydon-Matterface, bottom right: by Kathy Bland,
bottom left: by Vickie Heydon-Matterface; pp. 12–13,
by Vickie Heydon-Matterface; p. 14, Denise Vince
by Barbara Mason, Jim & Jeanne by Pat Best, Jane
Holmes by Steve Williamson, Jo Tyler by Karen Usher,
Linda Colson, Jenny Clarke & Michael Wenborn by
Karen Dunstan, Gill Betts by Jennifer Ross; all other
photos by BRF staff.

Printed in the UK by Stephens & George Print Group

Note for subscribers

Print copies are dispatched to arrive six weeks prior
to the date on the cover of the magazine. The January
2022 issue should be with you around the middle of
November 2021. The PDF version of the magazine is
also available for purchase and immediate download
from the beginning of November. messychurch.org.uk/
resources/get-messy

Photocopying for churches

To order back issues of Get Messy! and other Messy
Church resources, email BRF at enquiries@brf.org.uk
or telephone +44 (0)1865 319700.

Send in news, stories, photos and general enquiries to
our Messy Church administrator on +44 (0)1235 858238
or messychurch@brf.org.uk.

Meet our session writers for this issue

Mark and Jane Hird-Rutter are the Regional
Coordinators for Messy Church in British
Columbia, Canada. They have been working as
Messy Church leaders since 2009. They are both
retired.

Martyn Payne worked with
the BRF Messy Church
team until he retired in December 2017.
Bible storytelling, intergenerational mission and
ministry, and schools work are particular passions
of his. Martyn is a Messy Church trainer.

Sharon Sampson loves showing
all ages that being a Christian can be a fun
adventure! She runs church camp-outs, Easter
experiences and interactive prayer stations, hides
painted rocks around the village and in the last
couple of years has set up a Messy Church.

Leyla Wagner and **Marty Drake** are
from Huntington Beach, California. Marty serves as
the director of children, youth and family ministries
at Community United Methodist Church, Huntington
Beach. They have both been on
Messy Church teams since 2013
and are founding members of the
Messy Church USA Board, for which
Leyla is secretary and Marty is board
president. They are both Regional
Coordinators and Leyla is also a Messy Church
trainer.

Marty Drake

Leyla Wagner

Themes in this edition

In the UK schools go back in **September**, so the story of Bartimaeus
making a new start through Jesus' power of healing could be tied into
the new start of term. It's a wonderful story that many children and
adults will identify with – the determination to keep on shouting until
God hears us and not letting anyone else get in the way!

In **October**, when Halloween celebrations preoccupy many families, we
look at a time in Elijah's life when he was scared and feeling isolated.

November celebrates a lovely woman called Tabitha, a member of the
early church. But even more so, we celebrate the power of Jesus to
bring someone back from the dead through his followers. At a time of
year when we often remember people who have died, this story might
be a good time to celebrate the gift of eternal life that Jesus gives.

And in **December** many of us will be wanting to go all-out in a wonderful Messy Christmas celebration, after the dreary restrictions of Christmas 2020. Our Canadian writing team for December have brought some
great suggestions for activities. This might be a family's one chance to
hear the real story of Christmas, uncluttered by elves and Santas, jolly
though these are. Let's make the most of it!